Dorian Album

for STRING TRIO
(VIOLIN — CELLO — PIANO)

by HARVEY S. WHISTLER and HERMAN A. HUMMEL

CONTENTS

RUBANK®

HAL•LEONARD®
CORPORATION
7777 W. BLUEMOUND RD. P.O. BOX 13819 MILWAUKEE, WI 53213

Evening Song
(Abendlied)

1

Piano Accompaniment

SCHUMANN

Cantabile (In a singing style)

1140 - 30

2

Country Dance
(Landlicher Tanz)

Piano Accompaniment

BEETHOVEN

Semplice (In a simple manner)

Rubank, Inc., Chicago, Ill.

String Salutation

Piano Accompaniment

SEITZ

Rubank Inc., Chicago, Ill.

1140-30

Happy Holiday

4

Piano Accompaniment

BÖHM

5 Vienna Life

Piano Accompaniment

STRAUSS

Rubank, Inc., Chicago, Ill.
1140-30

Cielito Lindo

6

Piano Accompaniment

C. FERNANDEZ

Gaily the Troubadour

Piano Accompaniment

T. H. BAYLY

Con anima (With animation)

Rubank, Inc., Chicago, Ill.

1140-30

8   Waltz from H. M. S. Pinafore

Piano Accompaniment

SULLIVAN

Melody for Strings

9

Piano Accompaniment

RUBINSTEIN

Con amore (With affection)

Rubank, Inc., Chicago, III.

1140-30

10

Dream of Love
(Liebesträum)

Piano Accompaniment

LISZT

11   Jesu, Joy of Man's Desiring

Piano Accompaniment

BACH

    Rubank, Inc., Chicago, Ill.   1140-30

It Came Upon the Midnight Clear

12

Piano Accompaniment

R. S. WILLIS

Rubank, Inc., Chicago, Ill

13   Andante from Iphigenia in Tauris

Piano Accompaniment

GLUCK

Rubank, Inc., Chicago, Ill.
1140-30

14

Ave Verum

Piano Accompaniment

15 Silent Night

Piano Accompaniment

FRANK GRUBER

Rubank, Inc., Chicago, Ill.

1140-30

Dorian Album

for STRING TRIO
(VIOLIN — CELLO — PIANO)

by HARVEY S. WHISTLER
and HERMAN A. HUMMEL

PUBLISHED FOR:

Violin (First Position)
Cello (First Position)
Piano

7777 W. BLUEMOUND RD. P.O. BOX 13819 MILWAUKEE, WI 53213

Dorian Album

for STRING TRIO
(VIOLIN — CELLO — PIANO)

by HARVEY S. WHISTLER and HERMAN A. HUMMEL

CONTENTS

RUBANK®

HAL•LEONARD®

Evening Song
(Abendlied)

Cello

SCHUMANN

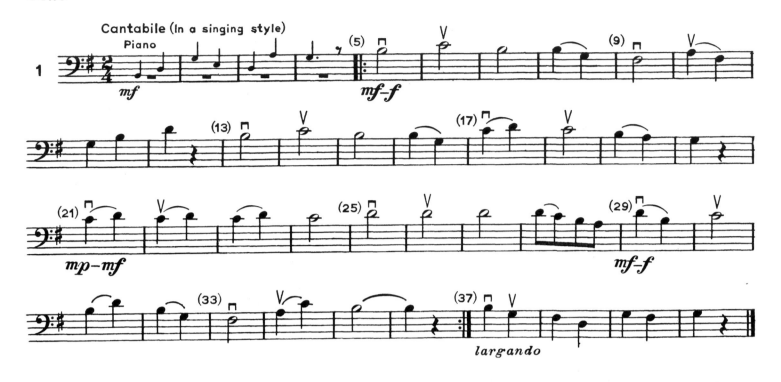

Country Dance
(Landlicher Tanz)

BEETHOVEN

1138 -15

String Salutation

Cello

SEITZ

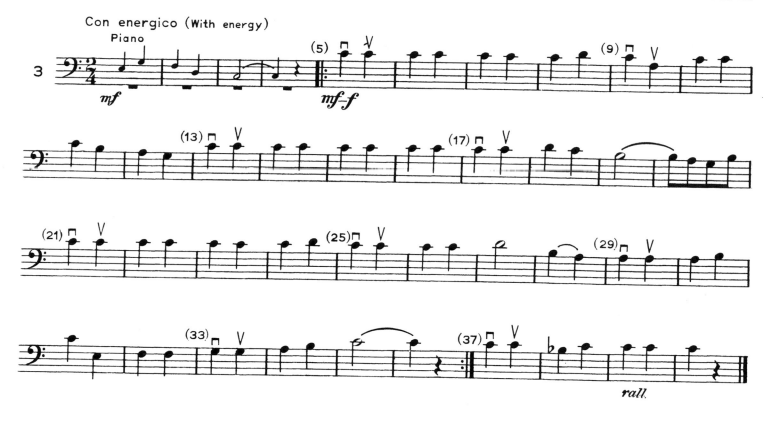

Happy Holiday

BÖHM

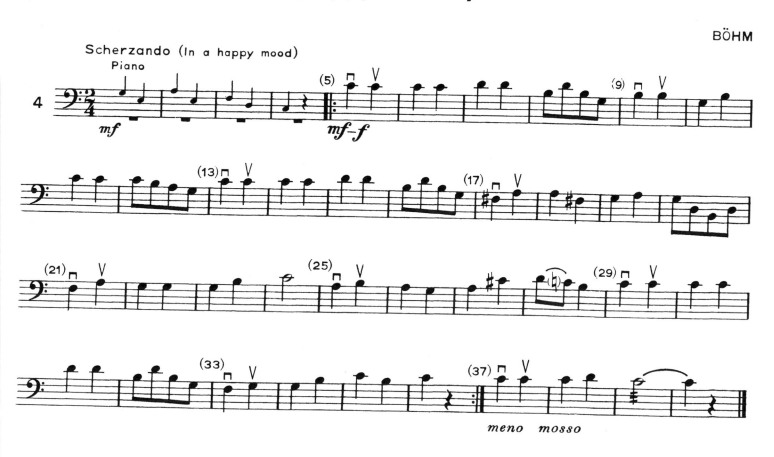

Vienna Life

STRAUSS

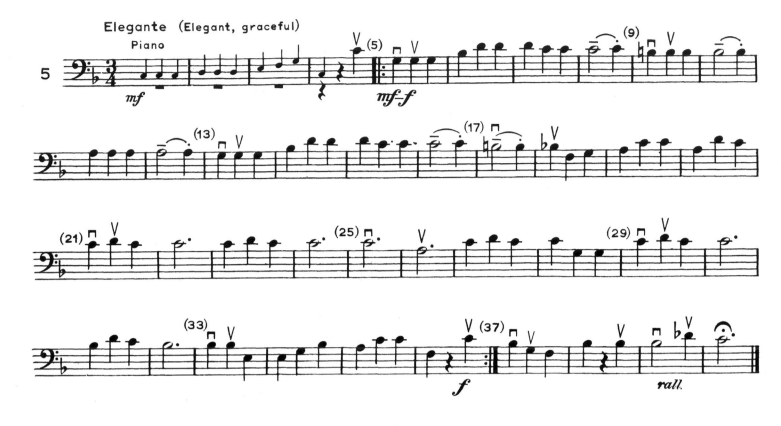

Cielito Lindo

C. FERNANDEZ

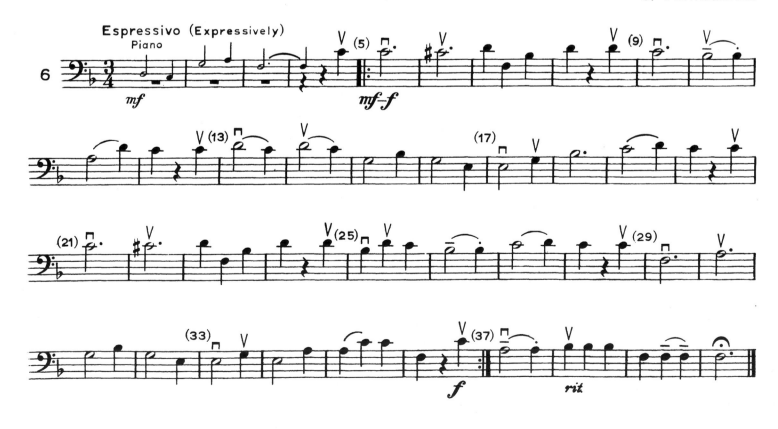

Rubank, Inc., Chicago, Ill.

1138 - 15

Gaily the Troubadour

Cello

T. H. BAYLY

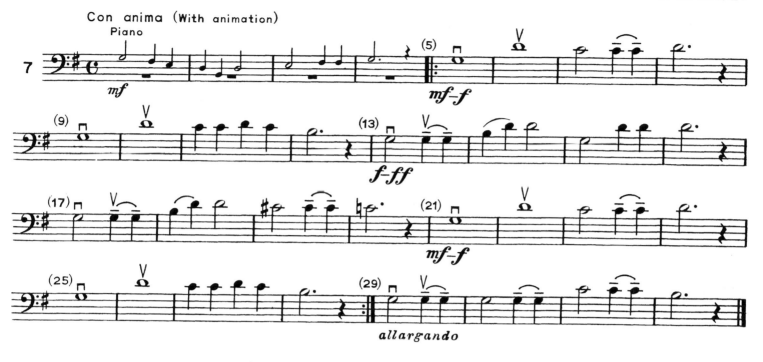

Waltz from H. M. S. Pinafore

SULLIVAN

Melody for Strings

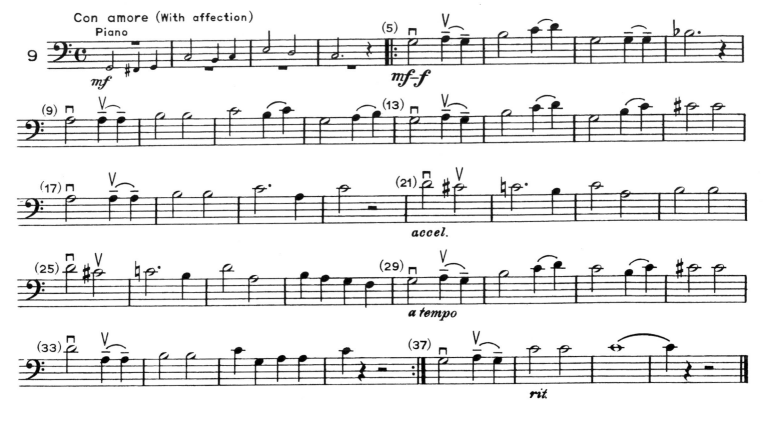

Cello

RUBINSTEIN

Con amore (With affection)

Dream of Love
(Liebesträum)

LISZT

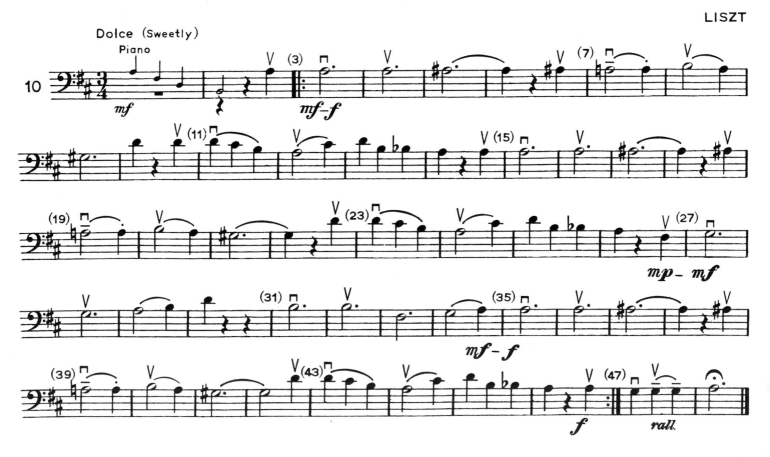

Dolce (Sweetly)

Rubank, Inc., Chicago, Ill.

1138 -15

Jesu, Joy of Man's Desiring

Cello

BACH

Religioso (Religious, devout)

It Came Upon the Midnight Clear

R. S. WILLIS

Con fervore (With fervor)

Andante from Iphigenia in Tauris

Cello

GLUCK

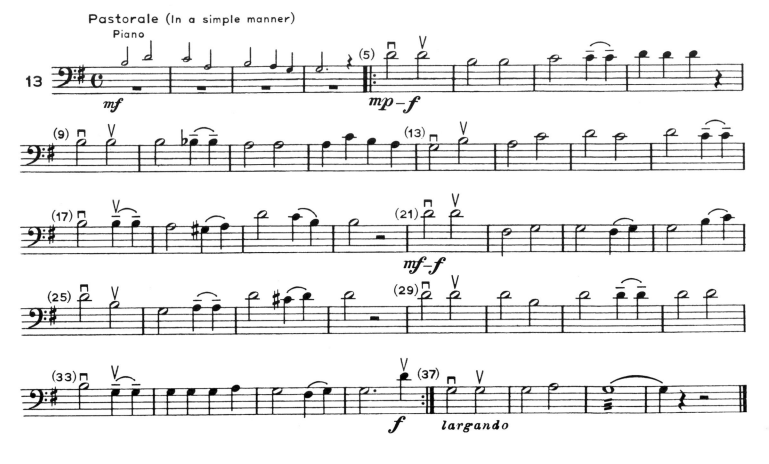

Ave Verum

MOZART

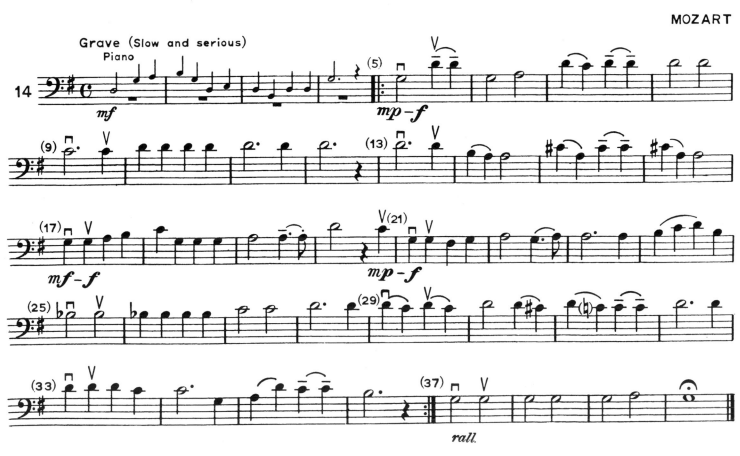

Rubank, Inc., Chicago, Ill.

1138-15

Silent Night

Cello

FRANZ GRUBER

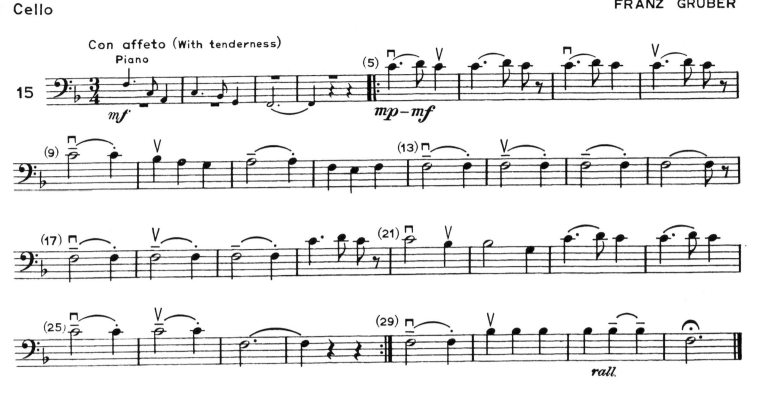

Drink To Me Only With Thine Eyes

Old English Ballad

Men of Harlech

Cello

Welsh Air

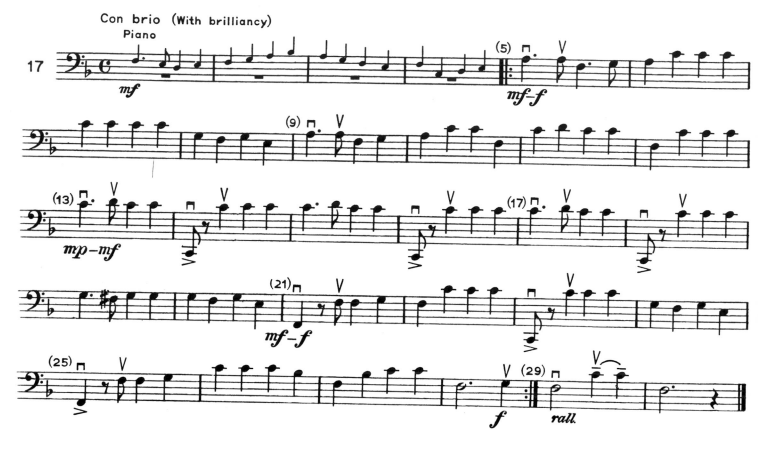

Alma Mater

School Song

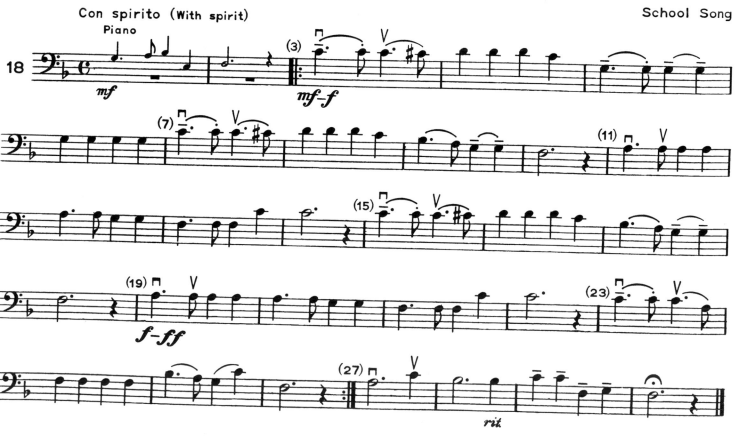

Rubank, Inc., Chicago, Ill.

1138-15

Theme from First Symphony

Cello

BRAHMS

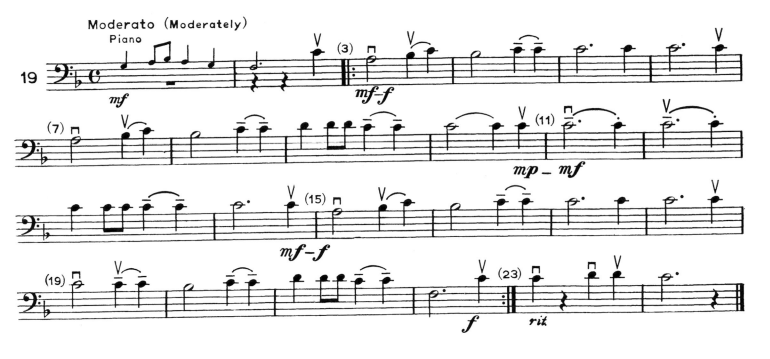

Excerpts from New World Symphony

DVORAK

Volga Boatman

Cello

Russian Folk Song

Con dolore (With grief)

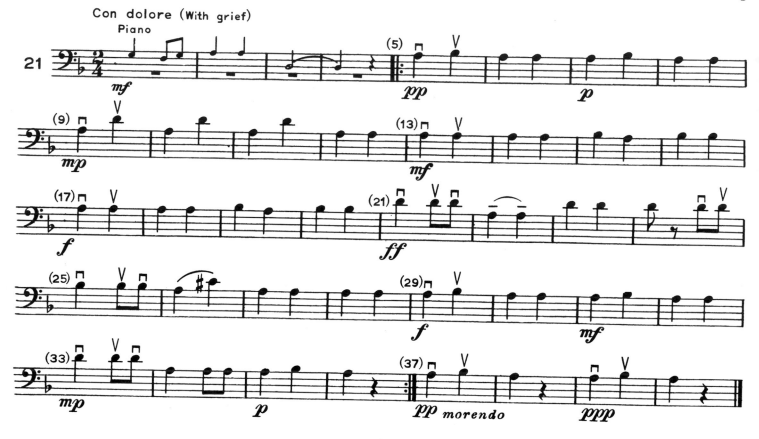

Jolly Coppersmith

PETERS

Allegro (Lively, quick)

Rubank, Inc., Chicago, Ill.

Oh! Promise Me

Cello

DE KOVEN

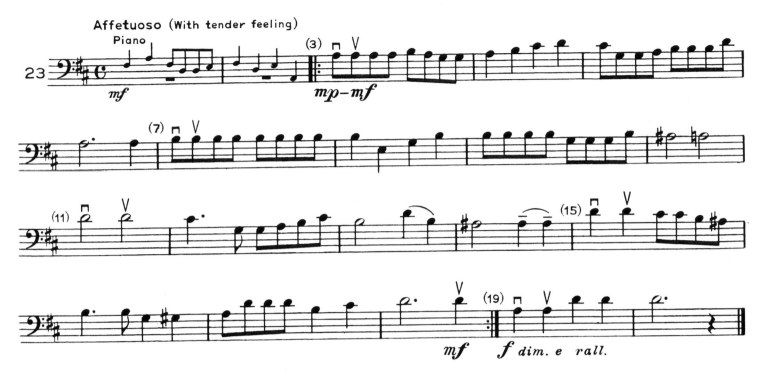

Rainbow Theme from Fantasie - Impromptu

CHOPIN

Rubank, Inc., Chicago, Ill.

Chanson Triste

Cello

TSCHAIKOWSKY

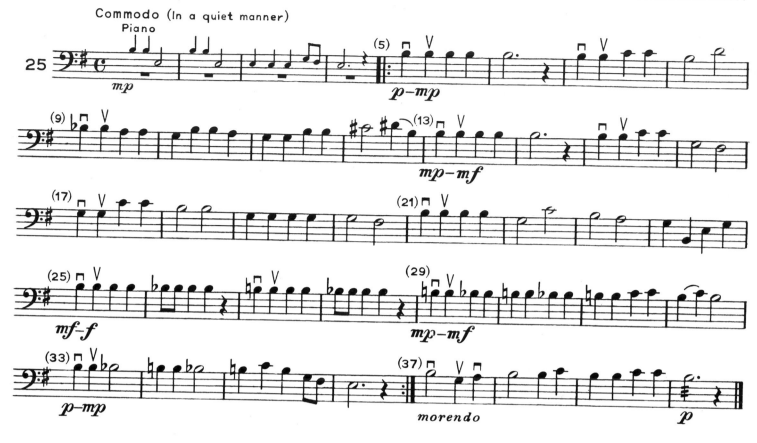

Menuet from Symphony No. 7

HAYDN

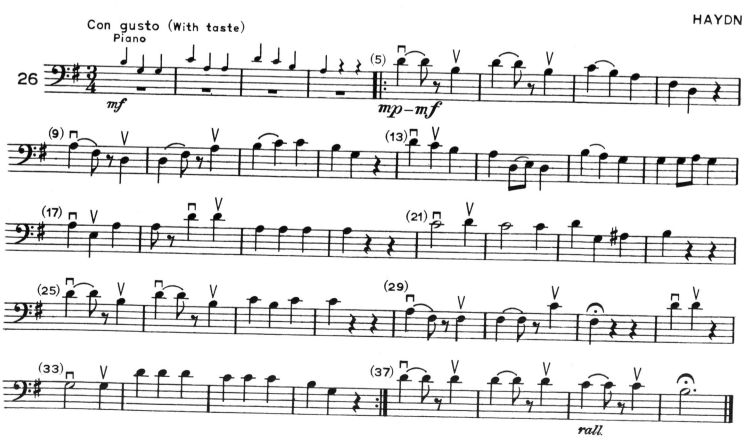

Rubank, Inc., Chicago, Ill.

Rondo from Sonata, Op. 137, No. 1

Cello

SCHUBERT

Carnival of Venice

Italian Folk Song

Rubank, Inc., Chicago, Ill

Allegro from Der Freischutz

Cello

WEBER

Processional Prelude

HANDEL

Rubank, Inc., Chicago, Ill.

1138-15

Dorian Album

for STRING TRIO
(VIOLIN — CELLO — PIANO)

by HARVEY S. WHISTLER
and HERMAN A. HUMMEL

PUBLISHED FOR:
Violin (First Position)
Cello (First Position)
Piano

7777 W. BLUEMOUND RD. P.O. BOX 13819 MILWAUKEE, WI 53213

Dorian Album

for STRING TRIO
(VIOLIN — CELLO — PIANO)

by HARVEY S. WHISTLER and HERMAN A. HUMMEL

CONTENTS

Rubank®

HAL•LEONARD®

Evening Song
(Abendlied)

1st Violin

SCHUMANN

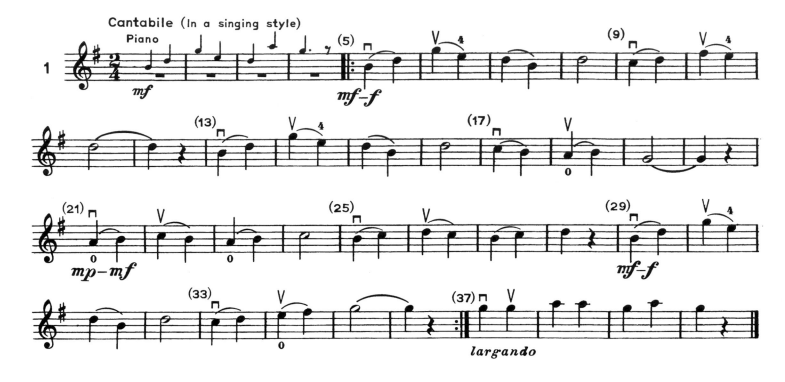

Country Dance
(Landlicher Tanz)

BEETHOVEN

1133-15

String Salutation

1st Violin

SEITZ

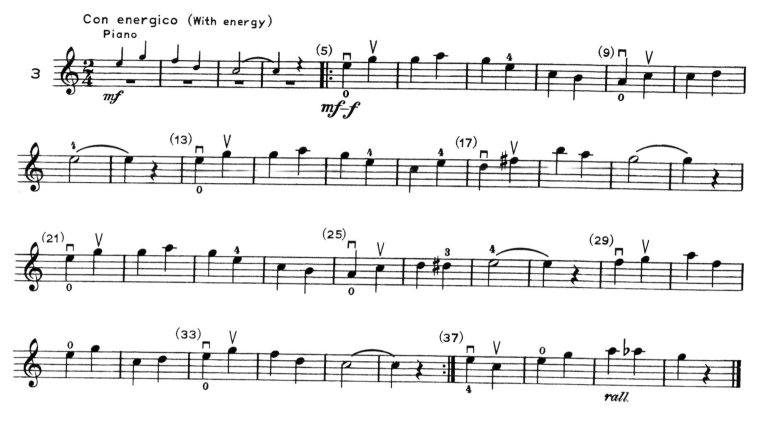

Happy Holiday

BÖHM

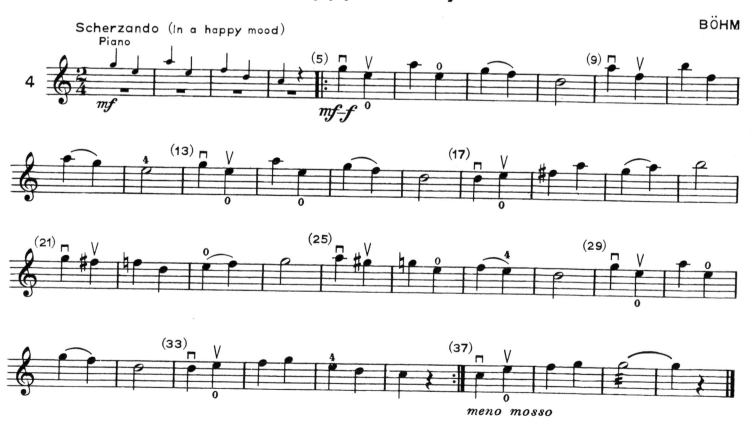

Rubank Inc., Chicago, Ill.

Vienna Life

STRAUSS

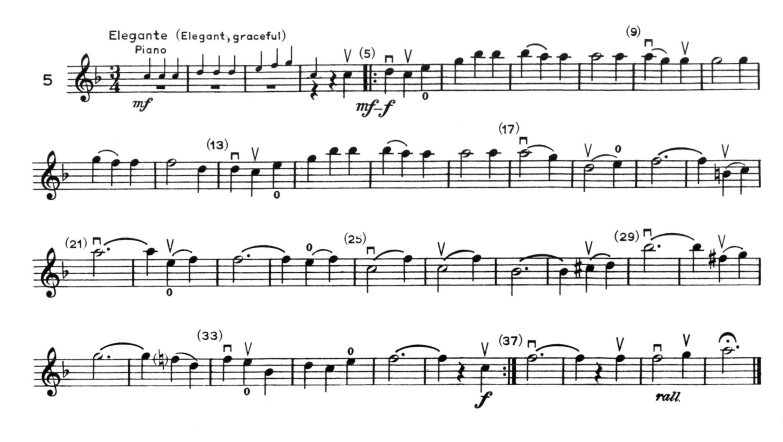

Cielito Lindo

C. FERNANDEZ

Rubank, Inc., Chicago, Ill.

1133-15

Gaily the Troubadour

1st Violin

T. H. BAYLY

Waltz from H. M. S. Pinafore

SULLIVAN

Melody for Strings

1st Violin

RUBINSTEIN

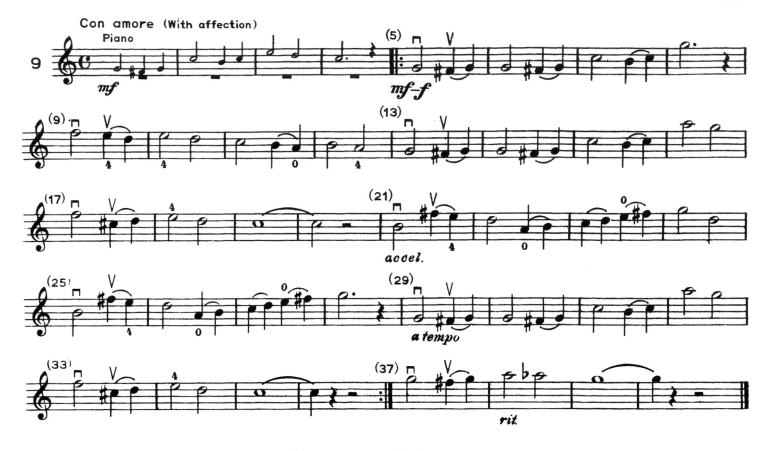

Dream of Love
(Liebesträum)

LISZT

Rubank, Inc., Chicago, Ill.

1133-15

Jesu, Joy of Man's Desiring

1st Violin

BACH

Religioso (Religious, devout)

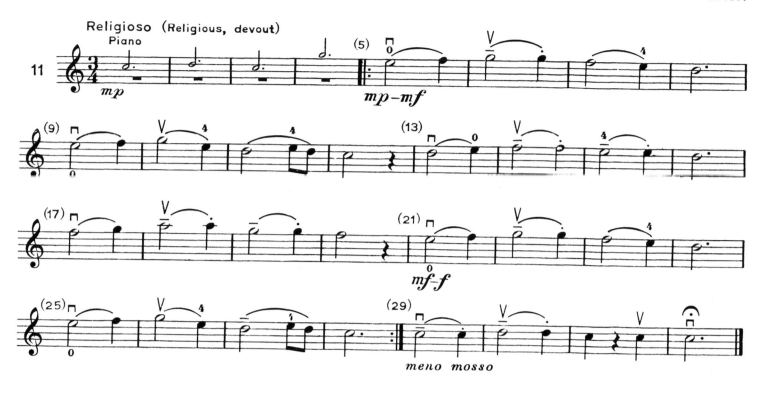

It Came Upon the Midnight Clear

R. S. WILLIS

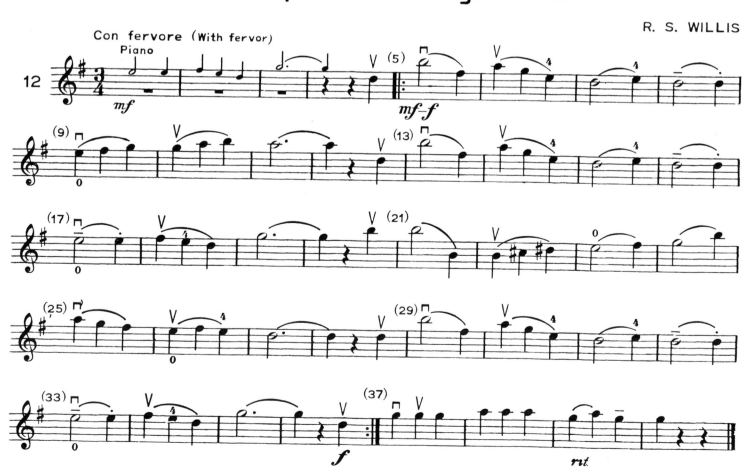

Andante from Iphigenia in Tauris

1st Violin

GLUCK

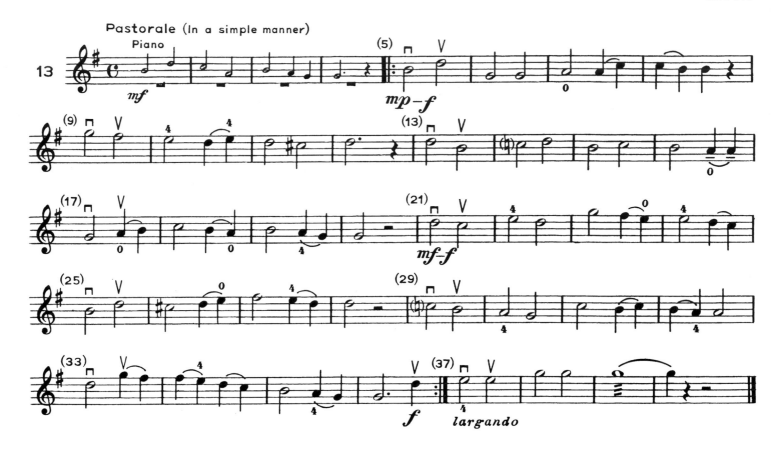

Ave Verum

MOZART

Rubank, Inc., Chicago, Ill

Silent Night

1st Violin

FRANZ GRUBER

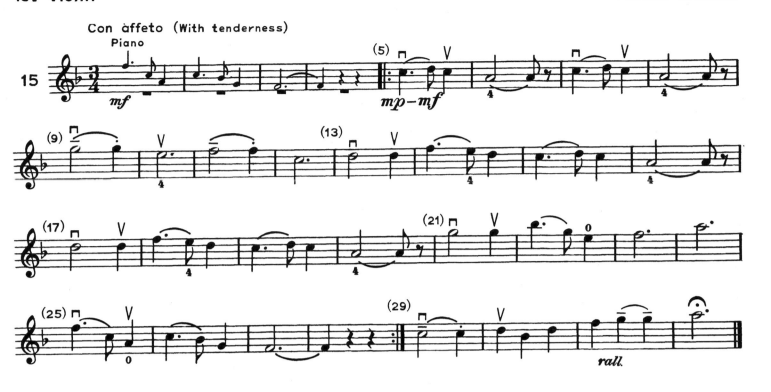

Drink To Me Only With Thine Eyes

Old English Ballad

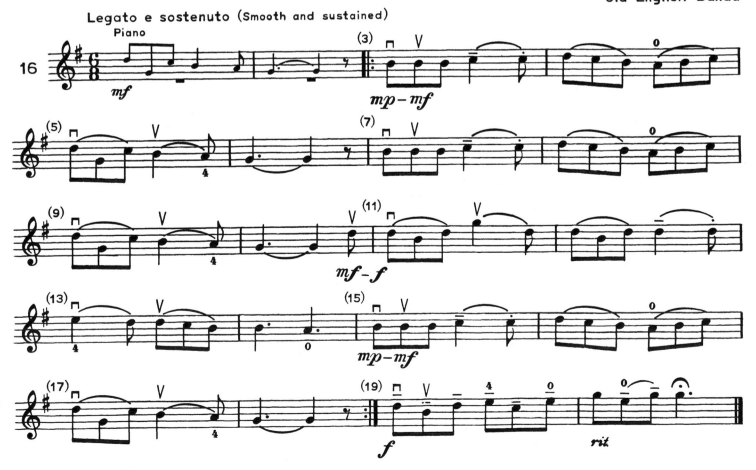

Men of Harlech

1st Violin

Welsh Air

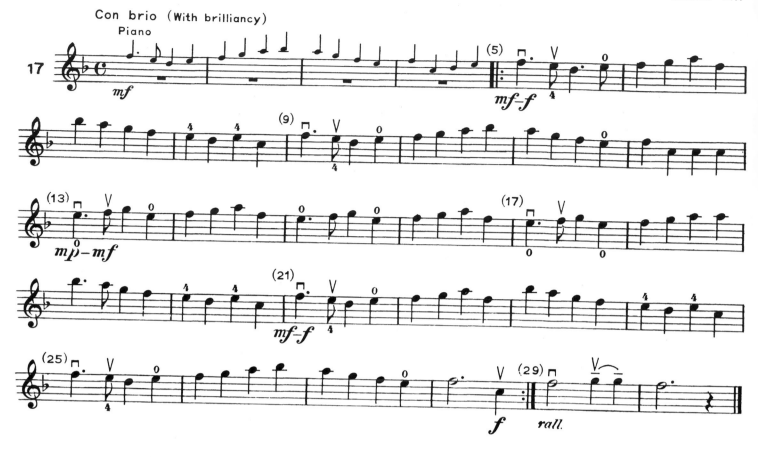

Alma Mater

School Song

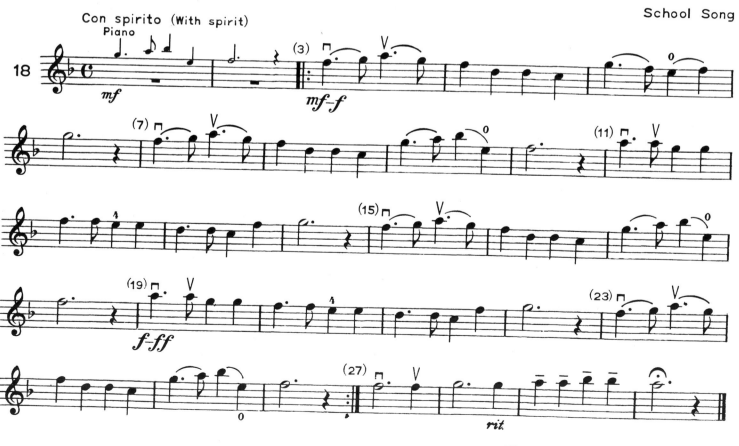

III.

Rubank, Inc., Chicago, Ill.

1133-15

Theme from First Symphony

1st Violin

BRAHMS

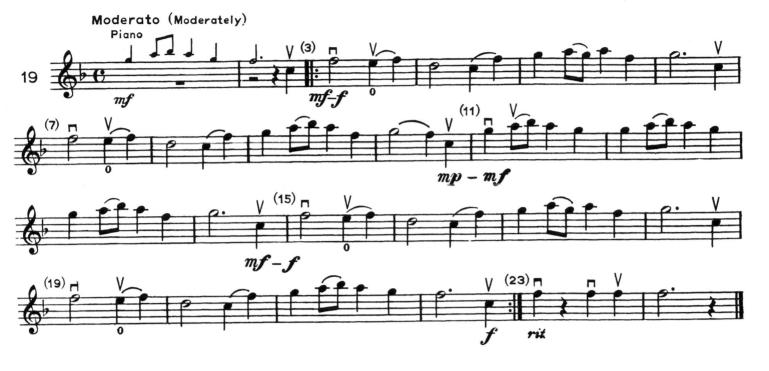

Excerpts from New World Symphony

DVORAK

1133-15

Rubank, Inc., Chicago, Ill.

Volga Boatman

1st Violin

Russian Folk Song

Jolly Coppersmith

PETERS

Oh! Promise Me

DE KOVEN

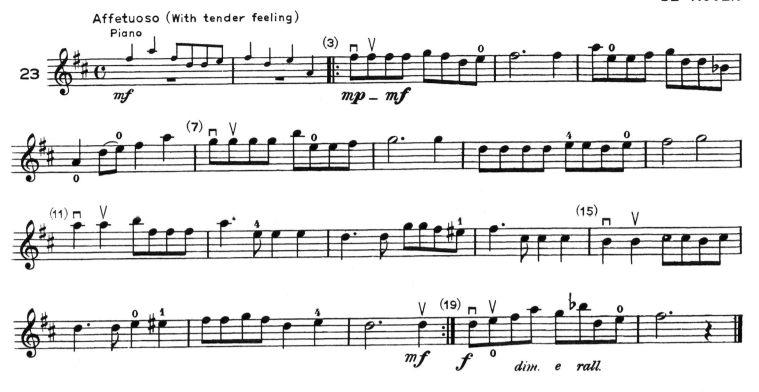

Rainbow Theme from Fantasie-Impromptu

CHOPIN

Chanson Triste

1st Violin

TSCHAIKOWSKY

Commodo (In a quiet manner)
Piano

Menuet from Symphony No. 7

HAYDN

Con gusto (With taste)
Piano

Rubank, Inc., Chicago, Ill

Rondo from Sonata, Op. 137, No. 1

1st Violin

SCHUBERT

Carnival of Venice

Italian Folk Song

Allegro from Der Freischutz

1st Violin

WEBER

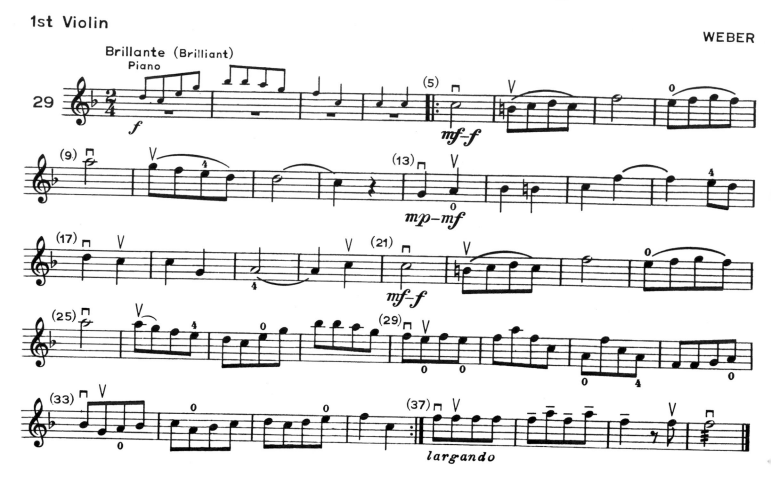

Processional Prelude

HANDEL

Rubank, Inc., Chicago, Ill.

Drink To Me Only With Thine Eyes

Piano Accompaniment

Old English Ballad

Rubank, Inc., Chicago, Ill.

17 Men of Harlech

Piano Accompaniment

Welsh Air

Con brio (With brilliancy)

Rubank, Inc., Chicago, Ill.

1140-30

Alma Mater

Piano Accompaniment

Rubank, Inc., Chicago, Ill.

19
Theme from First Symphony

Piano Accompaniment

BRAHMS

Rubank, Inc., Chicago, Ill.

1140-30

Excerpts from New World Symphony

Piano Accompaniment

DVORAK

Larghetto (Moderately slow)

Rubank, Inc., Chicago, Ill.

21 Volga Boatman

Piano Accompaniment

Russian Folk Song

Con dolore (With grief)

 Rubank, Inc., Chicago, Ill. 1140-30

Jolly Coppersmith

Piano Accompaniment

PETERS

Rubank, Inc., Chicago, III.

Oh! Promise Me

Piano Accompaniment

DE KOVEN

Affetuoso (With tender feeling)

Rubank, Inc., Chicago, Ill.

1140-30

24 Rainbow Theme from Fantasie-Impromptu

Piano Accompaniment

CHOPIN

Rubank, Inc., Chicago, Ill

25

Chanson Triste

Piano Accompaniment

TSCHAIKOWSKY

Rubank, Inc., Chicago, Ill.

1140-30

Menuet from Symphony No. 7

Piano Accompaniment

HAYDN

Rubank, Inc., Chicago, Ill

27 Rondo from Sonata, Op. 137, No. 1

Piano Accompaniment

Rubank, Inc., Chicago, Ill.

1140-30

Carnival of Venice

Piano Accompaniment

Italian Folk Song

Rubank, Inc., Chicago, Ill.

29   Allegro from Der Freischutz

Piano Accompaniment

WEBER

Rubank, Inc., Chicago, Ill.

1140-30

Processional Prelude

Piano Accompaniment

HANDEL

Rubank, Inc., Chicago, Ill